## Other titles in the UWAP Poetry series (established 2016)

## Praise for the first edition

These vivid poems meld wild energy with meticulous crafting. They trace the tactile, the remembered and the sensuous, tracking young lives as they unfold under a 'deadpan sky'. With their exquisite music, fresh and startling images, they are variously evocative, mournful and vibrant. They witness the gritty, the violent and the intense with unflinching focus, probing atonement and resolution as their histories rise and subside. This is an exceptionally assured and original debut.

**Felicity Plunkett**

Rico Craig's *Bone Ink* is an electrifying collection. From the lost legacy of a Malay childhood to star-crossed lovers in Sydney's Bella Vista Drive, Craig's characters court danger with grand desperation and an urgent desire to escape. Born of trauma and passion these poems strive to outrun their own destinies, deliquescing into painful and exquisite explorations of memory and nostalgia. Like shoes left dangling on powerlines or ghostly hand-prints cast into concrete, *Bone Ink* stamps its distinctive mark on the landscape of Australian poetry.

**Michele Seminara**

Urban, decadent, dystopian; in Rico Craig's Western Suburbs there are many countries, caliphates, Terracotta warriors and Arctic shelves. With 'the taste of a derelict future', his working-class songs and spells have a political consciousness that is unafraid to be mythopoetic. *Bone Ink* is a fine debut from a poet to watch, whose work has already crossed national borders.

**Michelle Cahill**

# Bone Ink

## Rico Craig

Rico Craig is a teacher, writer and award-winning poet whose work melds the narrative, lyrical and cinematic. Craig is published widely; his poetry collection *Bone Ink* was winner of the 2017 Anne Elder Award and shortlisted for the Kenneth Slessor Poetry Prize 2018.

*Bone Ink* was originally published in May 2017 by Guillotine Press, which went out of business in December that year. This edition features all the original poems and an additional 25 poems exploring the *Bone Ink* world.

# Rico Craig
# **Bone Ink**

First published in 2019 by
UWA Publishing
Crawley, Western Australia 6009
www.uwap.uwa.edu.au

UWAP is an imprint of UWA Publishing,
a division of The University of Western Australia.

Copyright © Rico Craig 2019
The moral right of the author has been asserted.
ISBN: 978-1-76080-109-0

A catalogue record for this
book is available from the
National Library of Australia

Inside front cover: the cover of the first edition of
*Bone Ink*, designed by Camille Walala
Designed by Becky Chilcott, Chil3
Typeset in Lyon Text by Lasertype
Printed by McPherson's Printing Group

 uwapublishing

for kv and pv

# Contents

## The Upper Room

# Bone Ink

# Angelo

We were the kids who hung shoes from power lines,
left them doubled in their swaying doom
to mark each steal. One of us worked the ignition

the other tossed twisting shoes at the deadpan sky
until they garrotted a line. As they swung
we eased into traffic, just another ducoed dream.

On the day he died we drove stolen cars
through the suburbs, spray cans knocking like eggs
in a swaying nest. I melted the dash & flicked

matches through the window.
From Parra Rd to Blacktown, our sweat mixed,
desperate, with the stink of scorched plastic;

& we sprayed mourning consonants on every
archway we found. *Cops Killed Tsakos*
& dash lights were our campfire, & in the fretful

lustre we might've been mistaken for men.
We gnawed on our tongues, smoked with acetone fingers
& we knew a stolen car was intent to murder,

to run. A weapon is what cops said; enough
for bullets through a windscreen.
*Cops Killed Tsakos*

At the funeral his mum howled her dark-haired
Greek rage. No one held her back, she ripped
the priest's cross off & threw herself

at the coffin. I can't go see her, no one visits
her now; when I'm home I drive past & imagine
her behind curtains condemning the TV

like a cursed queen. All she wanted was good boys,
like good boys could take him out of that car.
*Cops Killed Tsakos*

Tonight we've found a column shift; bench seat
relic from the empty streets of Granville. Something big
enough to hold us all, with air enough

for memories to breathe. It's rare. & we burn
the old roads, searching for the words we sprayed
on underpass vaulting. Artless black memorials.

& the night is full of letters fading, briefly
in our headlights. *Cops Killed Tsakos*
Soon we'll give up, drive to the BP near the corner

of Victoria & James Ruse; where they do the kebabs
Angelo liked. & we'll lean on the car, & listen
to traffic, & watch the safety lights spit insects,

& we'll feed his ghost.

# Blackberry Caliphate

For months men with coloured stakes have pegged the suburb,
subdivided their way over the hill, toward our hidden place,
this clutch of blackberry. We're here again, arms smeared

with sour fruit, hands nicked and bloodied from passage
through the bramble. Under our canopy there's a lull.
Over the hill a dozer sputters diesel; you've put sugar

in their tanks, delivered secret spells with sticky fingers
and your two-stroke tongue. Tricks don't hold long,
nothing works. They'll find us, out beyond

their kerbs and cul-de-sacs, gorging on sour berries,
licking the skin from our lips. You've stubbed
a midden of butts in silence. I need to act now.

There are leaves to pick from your hair; I kiss
the grease on your neck, your exhaust fume breath
buries the shape of words in my ear. I guide you

to me. Exhale your weight, until we're side by side,
in the musty dirt, damp on our shoulder blades, rabbit
eyes in the shadows. When we come in from the hills

our palms cling, sticky with blackberry; backs grass-slapped,
pin-pricked with bindis and briars. In the hours
we've been gone, they've poured cement between stakes,

mapped our sandstone heart with a concrete tattoo. The footpaths
shimmer; we walk, gravel dust at our ankles, until we find
a place to kneel and cast our hands in wet cement.

# Through the Witch Window

Soon I'll be lucent, at your witch window,
hand raised ready to knock. There are no lies

hidden between my toes; I am true
down to the soles of my three stripes. Tonight

I've been riding shotgun with my diamond-eared
brother. We've been a lime-green streak, Datsun clack

clack, under the cathode constellations of this city.
My head out the window, howling your name

into celestial alignment; we're satellite streaks,
orbital promise. The second summer of love

is in my veins, heart beating against my throat;
this is the last night you'll be

the daughter of teachers. Tonight we undo
all their plans; leave them snoring, mutton

counting in their dreams. We'll go
to Peats Ridge, watch harmonics shudder

the mist, dance ourselves toward firelight. I run
up your drive, past the rusted-out trailer. And

I'm at your window, hand raised.
You're at the glass before I knock,

bag on your shoulder, ready to straddle
the window; your hands around a jar,

all our half-hearts collected,
beating their slippery, faltering time.

# Emperor of 32 Bella Vista Drive

Terracotta Warriors guard their Emperor. Fifteen
archers in the al fresco dining area, a four-car garage
full of foot soldiers. The Emperor is damp
with middle age and dawn dew, askew

on a banana lounge, his dressing gown unhitched.
The High Chariot and team of bronze horses
spent in the master bedroom. Bins line the street,
neighbours sleep. Soldiers will decamp with the sun,

night shadows lost in the civil dawn; he'll miss them.
He's found affection for their sandalled feet,
learned to accommodate their placid foment. The sun
will rise over half-built mansions. His daughter

has not returned. There have been boys aiming rocks
at her window, quartz pebbles through the night air,
neat parcels of intent. The infantry have reported.
Secrets have passed through the ranks, a ragged, worried

line to his ear. She carries his devious blood. The only
heartbeats in this house belong to his wife and their dog
as it wanders between the ranks. They are a family shuffling
toward roundabouts, born in the first dust of subdivision.

His daughter has outgrown the suburban vista,
outlived artless childhood devotion, now a tussle twists
in every conversation. She rails against these ancient guards,
their empty hands, their ceramic topknots. They

are his alone. The troops bear eight faces of despair.
Rumours arrive hidden in sheafs of silk,
hugged in the dimple of lacquered bowls; cradled
by foot soldiers who lived through the nuclear birth,

The Long March, had their memories cleansed
by one hundred torrents of mercury. They say –
silver will bring gold, the canopy of wealth; still,
young love will arrive with a darkened tooth, a tattoo

behind the ear, a labourer's inflection. These desires
deboss the blood. He hefts himself from the banana lounge,
takes a step toward an archer, stands eye to eye
and tilts to kiss; holds his lips against the cool surface.

When he draws away there are flecks of ancient paint
on his lips, the taste of clay and fealty; these mute servants
are the body of another epoch. The morning birds start,
the swimming pool filter churns. He imagines kissing his wife

with terracotta lips; wonders if she will remember
his fingertips on her, each touch a scalpel of morning dew.

# Train Delays

Two decades wishing on wrinkles
turning down your smile. I had to be

prepared for the way you'd appear
to me, a furrowed addendum to clouded Kodachrome,

with a tie straight from the 90s,
belt a cinch too tight.

Our meeting doesn't match the script
I hate-draft every dawn. I catch the familial

shape your chin casts at morning.
School kids yell over one-eared music. You're under

the indicator board, it's scrolling
through stations, there are dead leaves

spilling from your pockets. I hear the rumour
as you hide your hands. A nursery rhyme I half remember.

I recognise the sound shapes make as they lose hold.
What you know of me

is on the concourse tiles: a coin,
some chewy wrappers, an apple core,

peach stone, a drink can, someone's lost
Opal card, a bundle of shoe laces. I didn't

know I was so many things
waiting to be scattered; all turned out

for you to discover,
me unreeling again, into this gulf of years.

# Monsoonal Light of Our Childhood

*Life cannot quell*
*thoughts of you my*
*brother*

In the Malay of childhood, you're eight,
our hands are sticky
with frangipani sap. It's rainy season;
you have starfruit juice, caught
silver on your chin,
the essence of a cloud.

Mum and Dad are playing paddle board
in the teeming rain, they're slick as orchids
swatting the downpour. My fingernails
are carmine tipped; I'm killing ticks,
our Alsatian whines. You run
into the rain, rambutans have fallen,
they're furred clots on the grass.

You're ten, Dad drives, a bottle of Bacardi
between his legs, Mum passes
him a tin of pineapple juice.
They trade slurps; Rita Coolidge sings.
We're in the backseat, tearing pastry
from curry puffs, nits crawling
through our hair. Brahmans linger
roadside and stare through the open window.
You reach, pining, toward
the rough warmth of their snouts.

You're fourteen, I ride the BMX you taught
me to strip and rebuild
to a house out the back of Kellyville.
The hash we score is ballast
in our lungs. We smoke it
at the soccer oval mesmerised
by the silhouette of a servo at sunset.

You're twenty-three
we're selling for Uriati, acid
in our pockets, felt under our fingers,
horses racing in our ears, laughter
sharp as a clattering break. He tells us
to deal with latex gloves, we don't listen.
Our nights are manifold,

never-ending, they wear the shellac
from our fingers. As you slip
the shackles of fear, I winnow,
prone with worry, and our night-years
flood my mouth with the taste of a derelict future.
I run from our suburban notch; cast off
to monsoonal Malay light
for a lost legacy. There's nothing. A place,
a past, no home. I return, years spent
without your trumpet voice,
scant comfort to offer.

You're twenty-eight
there are boards over the windows;
you're bare to the waist watching
words in the trees.
My car twists down the dirt track;
you speak of buried money, angry spittle
on your lips, a scalp
cropped in rage, your muscles
taut as bones, unloaded gun
in your hand.
I am the key for your curse. You
let me lock you away
in a room with men who tend and bridle

the anger between your teeth,
the fire in your spine,
men who watch you sleep, who know
how the hidden blade cuts. I'm thirty the last time
your lips score the air with my name
the last time
I see the voice of our mother in your eyes.

# Kuala Lumpur 1977:
# Prawn Heads, Oil Rigs and Infidelity

Fourteen on seven off, incessant
equatorial days, heavy city sky, tarps dripping
on stall counters. Prawn heads underfoot,

exo-crunch on concrete floors. Bare bulbs,
the bright lights dangling, threaded by mosquitoes.
Two rig workers lift steel tins of Anchor beer

and chew prawn flesh. They're silver-palmed,
thick-tongued, slick-skinned, the pernicious few
riding a state of expat grace. Woks steam,

surrounded by tins, tubs of grease
and ponds of chicken blood. Reedy men
in singlets sweat, exhaling strands of smoke,

working the woks as ash falls through
their arms. The chilli-fingered oil man
clutches a photo, bent, battered by his wallet:

a woman, shirtless, dark hair, haloed
in a rattan chair. All he says is, *look at her
how could you not trust her?* His friend

doesn't turn, nodding wordless sympathy;
eyes on the wok-steam rising, disappearing.
The photo is thrust again, a shivering fist,

he looks, doesn't speak, caught by
the hurry of mortality punching in his chest.
*Look at her, she won't tell me who it is!*

Blinkless, she stares from the photo
divine as a gecko, tail part-shed, scaling a wall.

# Tropical Storm Danielle: Night Surfing

Headline from *Corpus Christi Caller*, 6 September 1980,
'Eight Dead as Danielle Hits Coast'


Kids with wetsuits and one eye
on the weather. We know nothing
like stealing a wave from the night;

with the winds of Danielle, good
breaks surge. At Mustang Island
we cut across a dune lip. The wind lifts

soft sand, our headlights play, caught
on the granules, and we drive blind
to the water edge. Waves rise

from the darkness and streak night
at our feet. You're first in the water.
Through binoculars, I watch the golden

light of oil rigs, holes in the storm-
mural-Gulf we propel ourselves against.
The darkness sucks you out. Sand

flays our jeep. I'm drawn to the gleaming
rig windows, their burley of distant alliance.
Through my lens the lights begin to twist

awry, canting from their suspended perch;
in two waves a cluster of windows topple
from the pylon. Golden light splayed;

no turmoil from the shore, only
a close constellation disturbed. I stand
and tilt the spotlight out to sea, waiting

for you to slide along the wall of a wave.

# Thane
## part 1: Jasper Road

Word on Facebook is you died in a field of mud
sword in hand
bellowing at the inevitable.
That's fake news.
Animals turned from your path,

birds hooked toward trees,
insects dropped their wings.
I heard you were housebound for years,
anxiety's leg-chains clunking as you prison-walked
down hallways. In the end

the only wishes in your lungs were carbon monoxide,
the only shapes you trusted
were daggers. You lavished thoughts
on empty spaces, collected wings fallen from cicadas,
filled your drawers with Dead Kennedys T-shirts;

your only ally had no limbs –
all wheels, torque and escape's punctured muffler.
A place to hole-up waiting for someone to slink beside you
test their palm on the handbrake and
talk to you like it was possible to be afraid

of the same things. Tomorrow broke into prophecies.
Three hags at the creek said your name.
You couldn't pick the difference
between your mum and your sister.
You thought we were all plotting behind our hands.

You were right about some things; our youth
promised like the hags. You believed the air
in their mouths, their riddles rattled
into another riddle. It wasn't the sword that killed you
not the curve taken too fast; each child leaves

an empty womb. We're born with mystic
voices in our ears, screeching like a fistful of cicadas.
Birth trills from open hands. Vibrating,
prophecies with wings; every word
the hags have spoken has colour,

thorax and eyes that cut the world to hexagons.
They see your car concealed in a closed garage,
doors locked, exhaust piped in a window,
your head nodding toward the steering wheel,
and every seventeen years they sing for you.

# Bonfire

I built a bonfire in his belly
and I'm burning our bones.

It's cavernous in here, there's no light,
no stars, no moon;

instead of squalls,
the sound organs make,

the breath, the heartbeat,
rivers of blood complicating his fingers

the intra-body mumble
his voice makes around me.

I'm terrified when he laughs,
that's rare

and I can see it coming,
an eclipse of thought, the ballooning red hills.

If we touch one another now
it's with air.

I'm below the bulge
his heart makes. There's heat beneath

stretching flesh. Memories
prowl at the edge of the bonfire

part-feral creatures not sure where they belong.
They're listening to warmth

waiting for the hiss of what was.

# Riot Control/Public Order

from Sarah Pickering's *Public Order*

nightly reconnaissance
                    north of the Thames
                        past Finsbury bustle
                        beyond lifers hoarding wine in Crouch End cellars

            insurrection on the breeze
        a broken window
                    murmurs at the all-night cafe
                            torching the populace to unrest

                                through the wire fence
                                over cinder blocks
            adrift across Farrance St

                police rehearse
                kettling manoeuvres
                    they plot to secure a barricaded shop front
                prepare gauntlets
                shoulder shields
                issue militaristic squawks

                    float past Lola Court
        back streets cut by barricades      abandoned cars
                            windows boarded
                                pubs frigid    and deserted

        look for messages in the phone box
                                near Eastcourt Street
                stories in the air    lovers lips

in the wind

they don't exist


on the plastic seats of the Rose Rd Social Club

there's an MC

a magician

first harmony of a love song

an invisible face hewn by the bristle of a rough kiss


wrap a coat around

the voices

wait at the Club        eat with fingers

try to remember the taste of Irn-Bru


police are at the door

every night


pounding


tromping stairs at Magdalen Green


always start

rat trap quick

when they batter through the front door

sometimes they come with commands

sometimes with arcane hand signals

and stomping feet

carry the pitch of atrocity

into this empty space

                    they number walls with targets
            spread and check rooms

furniture is a collection of skeletons
        nailed to the floor
            voices are the magician's flourish
                    enemies        a cloak's swirl

        they herd ghosts
                        black boots through shadow
                        gauntlets swing
                        truncheons at light
            the dust is trampled into movement

            police withdraw    formations dissolve      High Street is still
        Victoria Street empty     grass grows through open doors
                    starlings unbraid euphoric intentions

    revolutions drift door to door    flame guttering in transparent chests
                    they holler in the hills
                            they throng    clothed in leaves and grass
                    chanting dissent's next murmuration

# August 28, 1988

circling planes have shot holes     in clouds        cast
cities to cinder              winged cylinders weighted
sonic echoes       the crowd below          flourishing
polity's pointed finger      gape through tarmac haze
sunglasses      bridged on the scent of fuel      tongues
twitch        armaments promise       twinkling at first
until a formation splits                       out of time
the spear of flight disturbed      a ridge in the sky
metal knifing                    rivets        a piece of sun
cast loose on        the sublunary      fire and molten
shrapnel         this furnace                       opens
a mantle       and bawls                              justice

# Hamburg

If anyone asks I will say, you are oceans away,
afloat in the ventricles of a great city's heart,
your fractious brain pecking the afternoon press,

your relentless devices compelling you toward
a smokey eyelet. I will say there is enough left
to summon. The Rathaus must be dripping

ice, rock salt strewn on our streets of Sternschanze.
I hope you've crunched some pale messages
for me. Friend, I'll remember you dancing

with shadows, your metal button words,
your argot-tipped tongue. All the deserted
cousins of who we are in bars we'll never return to,

salt-lipped communards dancing in *Flaktürme,*
intemperate almost-selves, gadfly hearts
wandering with snow in their hair. Selves

always in transit, mirror fictions,
identity cast from their pockets; let them be
always as they are. I'll tap my toes

in secret on our ring of smoke. If we meet again
it will be unexpected, as will-less shoppers,
caught lingering in front of a cheese cabinet,

shocked, seeking salvation in a slab of brie.
We'll both be empty handed, shoeless,
one sock lost in the tide and the breaths we share

will be stained with the silt of industrial cities,
the taste of places bright enough to burn sand into glass.

# A Cheekbone For You To Climb Over

There were nights you ate grass,
just because it was cold and the taste
reminded you not to smoke;

carried tufts in your pocket to chew
as we drifted place to place in mini-cabs,
meditating against the cold. Nothing is solid,

we are as transparent as the terraces,
our boots empty; most of what we know
holds court in the first light morning tricks

over the nearest horizon. In night's huddled afterburn
you'd be lifting green threads
from between your teeth. Blathering magnificent

secrets; you talk too fast and too Southern French
for me to believe a word. You'd fill your head
with smoke and scream,

but it sounded like – 'If you touch my face again
I swear
when we walk down the street people

will see a chorus line.
Twenty of us kicking
in a half-moon.' I still don't know

what you were trying to make us understand,
if there were nights when this address
was the only thing between us

and tomorrow. I remind myself,
nobody knew enough to say it would be
okay, we were too busy building monuments

in stairwells, waiting for keys to arrive.
In my mind there's a blue room, a table between us,
winter sun pledging through the window,

a water heater clicking in the background
and you
searching for a coat you don't need.

# Spaniards Road

Today I'm glad

        I didn't know
        you'd die in this place

               and this squally city
                 would fill with
                       enemies.
              They follow me
                 vulture-hulking
                 on the tube
                 crow-eyed on this bus

          we ride.

     210 westward

   along Spaniards Ridge

             into the veil.
             Both black sheep and blustery
             we disembark
                walk, laugh; this is ours.

          Cutting jagged
        down an oak lined
            dirt path.
             In bushes beat hung –
      worn rubber. Slippery

voices in twilight jesting
                    a weight on each branch.

          We laugh knowing.

They'll find you here
          battered through bruising,
                    walletless, unnamed

                    for days
                              unclaimed.

     I'm glad
I didn't know. Today,

                    we make it through

                         ragged-leafed sessile
     to a grassy spur, sky free
               where the heath falls away.

          We stop

                              deep in grass
          and lower to haunches
     then knees, wordless.
We cross

struts, tuck fabric
      check rubric, uncertain
            until frame and cloth

                            are tethered.

              And the string is yours. I've the kite
        to my chest for a lifting moment
wings beating like a baby heart.
            The wind rises, you're floating
across grass, string unfurling
                henna wild, tacking for
      brief eloquent buoyancy.

## Streets Have Shadows

Yesterday evening you returned to me,
in front of Medici's, walking pale,
bent, a slipshod plait hanging from white
unruly hair. Nails crimping the plastic off
a pack of Lambert and Butler, your
picket lips puckering for a drag.

I know you from the gutter edge,
hardly twenty, in Auburn, brawling
for a cigarette, kicking
a car that wouldn't start,
throwing keys across the road.

Now your eyes are rheumy, trapdoors
over the sump-hole you tended
so well. I hear a mutter
as you rest between each step.

Your gimcrack dress billows, green
and threadbare, a grandmother's
cast-off. I watch your broken gait.

You grin, toothless; gentle
a smoke between your lips,

happy as a child.

# Unco Guid in Elthorne Park

Cast ashes adrift. A past never
said, confessions rippling
on the breeze, crumbling black, tumbling
into the park's feckless noise. Cider
drinkers and skater-kids will be first

witness. Hidden pictures
all bent by ratty devotion. They
smell of strange houses
and a husband's breath.
In the fire: a ring,

a black wedding dress, grim
happiness, a Germanic
bird of prey espying
mortal danger ahead. The Unco Guid
is loud. Fire doesn't cleanse

impiety. Easter will be here
soon and none have strength
to face the eternity stalking. This park
is hell enough. The ring is off,
pictures ash. It's not enough,

there's no sanctuary until the past has been
annulled and we kneel
to confess the human shreds
we've tied in godly laces.

# What I Should Have Said

Every lover leaves for a bed of insects,
for the sound of roaches
squabbling over blood.

There's the shadow of clouds, the smell of old jasmine.
Anyone could fall
through this gap. The wind comes in,

window frames tumble onto the street.
Each breeze is a shudder-memory playing
through wooden blinds. Every lover breathes cracks

in the pavement; people are sequestered in doorways,
tied in knots under tables.
There's nothing delicate about an ending;

horned insects scratch an essay into thighs.
And in the trees there are no birds
only the coats lost

hanging now –
hollow arms pressed.

## Guitar for Sale:
## Gretsch White G6136T – $4000

sleeping babies are the grist threshed from every dawn
wasted listening as foal-legged boys
strummed guitars and packed cones

now lusts are plastic toys
recorded lullabies fill the air
cots are hived in afternoon sun
the babies have names not words

one of the Rubys has turned
there's a nightmare under the film of her eyelid
my head is full of first aid training

resuscitation face shields
plastic lips
they're all breathing
the pre-verbal don't bother with excuses

they're here everyday
crying when they want and kecking at the sky
i ferry kids into the arms of parents

they juggle the laptop
they unhitch their top button
i have owl's wings painted on my cheeks
and i don't think

i'll remember to wash them off before
i leave
i'm wondering if there's track work again

tonight on the South Coast Line
if i'll be busing it from Hurstville
and i'll get to doze over the freeway
if i'll be able to get home late

exhausted enough to sleep
without turning on a light
so i

don't have to talk to the Gretsch hunched in the corner
and make another threat
to sell it on eBay
people couldn't guess the bid i'm waiting for

all those frets know too much about his hands
and the urgent 4/4 pressure it takes to play
our chorus into an infant chest

# Arrhythmia: Near the Pool Table at the Commercial Hotel, Saturday Night, Braidwood 1996

It's Braidwood winter, ice in every breath; my girlfriend
is in love with the guy singing Donna Summer covers.
He'll die before we do – misadventure,
the coroner won't count the pills floating in his stomach.

I get why she wants to leave. I've been wearing
white gloves to bed, fingers filled with a cream that will stop
my skin splitting. I perform a mime every night
before we sleep. All she ever does is listen.

On the makeshift stage he's gyrating like there's a future
he can enjoy. I've known him since we were kids.
All his moves are a waste.
The place is filled with weekenders from Canberra

and exes who haven't been able to cut
the pull of this town. He's drifting
with poisonous insects, dancing away
from the stingers. For now he's quick enough,

but it won't last. I almost feel for him,
lightness hurts to lose. Before the decade is out
he'll be scoffing over-the-counter meds and throwing
bourbon bottles at cars. Tonight he's breathing

different air, poised to unravel,
shedding this town like a tainted skin.
Youth's centripetal force is the only thing
holding us together.

My girlfriend is almost a nurse, in twenty years
she'll be deregistered for biting a hunk of flesh
from her husband's face. She'll lose years roaming
the single-lane highways of the Central West

pockets loaded with concrete chips. We don't have
a clue how patient the future is;
grey beards and addiction,
even children won't have the strength

to right us. Lately I've been waking in hotel rooms,
my boots in the corner, the sound of country
out the window. I've started counting the trucks
as they pass, like there's a message in the gaps,

it feels like that's always been where I didn't look.
There must have been hints of us
in the silence. My heart has lost hold of who we were
going to be, it barely has the will to keep time.

He sings Donna Summer lyrics like a decree,
elongating the moment under each word.
I watch, it could be aimless fun,
but every now and then there's a double beat

for him
and her
for the thought of what the two of them
might have been.

# in any city, in every tongue, we walk toward the heat of morning

tyres spinning
a face in the window yawning abuse
grown men grip boredom in fists

traffic lights change
feet in tangled unison
a milk crate kicked

the street fills with tatters
voice

peals of light
streamers caught on shoulders and carried

trailing colour

future spills onto Bourke Street
wearing glitter shorts
a feathered headdress

the lost child of a thousand incandescent gatherings

i've been sleeping at a bus stop
briefly
to catch my sense before daylight

an intoxicated logarithm
the pinpoint dance

                                    a satellite tracks above the sky
                      fine-tuned geometry of a courting ritual

        i hear a car gunning

                            toward the red light

                        i see

                                        a bottle telling its arch story
                        to the dawn air

            there's two lifetimes
                    in the way light contorts on glass
                    in the dazzle i see
                                    every bed we share
                each laceration preserved

# Life Savers

We're trapped in this vodka decade,
battered by the aftertaste of Skinny Bitches,
lime between our fingers, septums
scraped raw, my Burberry scarf
louche around your neck all summer.

You're so Sid Vicious you make
the cyber-dykes swoon. Your tongue
is a luxury car sweeping around
a manicured hedge, your lips taste
like spirit poured from a crystal skull.

I'm on your trust fund diet. We've
been talking to the warehouse doctor;
chicken, pork and Life Savers
the only food that'll pass our lips. Each
dawn you pace the gritty floor barefoot,

searching for the right pill. You push me
to my knees so we can make another
bullshit narcotic pact. We're full of holes,
but I promise anyway, something
about being beaten clean with sage bush,

drinking ouzo and being weathered
by salt air. I lie and listen to the birds
that roost in the roof above, they coo
at the empty din rushing from our bodies.

# Train to Quakers

I am a ghost coming home. The dove
on your wrist has turned to ash. No song
will bring you back. Old awnings and their flaking

messages bewilder me; the sound of a siren
in front of Red Rooster, slow changing traffic lights
where I cupped your head as you fell

into an electric riddle; your epileptic body
in desperate shapes on the pavement. I still
feel your shaved scalp against my thumb,

hear the ticking of bangles as you shake
visions from your fingers, see the pitch of your
eyes turned back. Those days were a gift.

My memory is pale witness to the sight of you
twisting on a bed, a cigarette burn by your right breast,
this young mind an ember in your hands. Today

has found all our secret rendezvous. I can taste
your Winfield Reds and hear the spindle of your
lighter scratching. I left these memories, years ago;

bundled in a waterproof jacket beside the train line
to Quakers, under a mound of rocks, never to be
retrieved. Now the hidden part of me that plucked colours

from your bird ribs is alive again. The dancing shadows
have returned, our gaunt teen desires are on their feet.

# Lysergic Triptych

**Panel 1**

                    second summer of love
                 with our dealer
                 a battle-axe
                   our class A
                 half-arsed banter

                    while he bagged
rolled
         gloved fingers
triple twenties

                  always started
                   on our fingers. He
drank beer from tins and swore
                           Each house

## Panel 2

We played
endless games
on the blade

                        manners,
                                 precision darts

- 501, 501, 501 -
       the barrel of his favourite
rubber
            Three games

                              with arithmetic
lessons and chalk dust
                               was the future,

all we cared about

## Panel 3

       all through

           hidden

         off Jasper Rd. Months

spent

preparing our

              tabs and doves,

            darts between

     fingers

          before we were allowed

to escape. Friday nights

                 owned dogs,

          Shoegaze

        were the Roses

# Thane
## part 2: Cicada Wings

They say the youngest child dies
on a Sunday. I wish I'd beaten more time
into your chest. Our twenties were carved from dust;

a decade living casual, lugging bubble-wrapped computers,
drinking gin from Solo cans while we waited
in loading bays for delivery trucks to arrive.

The best nights were spent in parked cars, telling lies
to shoestring glamours with tatts on their wrists;
they held your face like a stolen knife.

You collected friends, hoarded each breath
in your shoebox full of cicada wings.
You told me we were all insects caught in stone,

preserved between layers of rock. You'd open
the box, get me to hold my hand close,
palm above, and tell me how their fascination with air

kept you alive nights. No one will say what happened
to you. It's hard. Your mother is a broken cigarette,
gummy eyes, a menagerie in her chest.

She poured the best part of her memory into your heart,
it wasn't enough to keep you straight.
For two days she's been sitting with Aunty June,

down your street, they're wailing
into crying towels, rags around their necks
drenched in tears. They've cried scar trails

into their chests. When boys die, she wants them
to be reborn, slippery, as men,
incisor missing, blood on their chin.

They've stopped saying your name, all
they do is croon baby sounds. And me
and the girls are down by the creek

with flashlights, stamping thunder from the ground,
trying to find a place for you and all your wings.

# Reunion – Our Suburban Lingua

Where are you? I've scoured this reunion; lost friends
huddled at the Bowling Club, caught in Keno Limbo,
feeding their last twenty into the hurdy-gurdy
pokie whir. It seems like old times. The best lives bewildered

among blinking lights; shucked, eyes
ready to spin, lips gold-pursed poised to gush
shiny confessions. Your friends strut
like fathers in driveways, pretending not to recognise;

but for a moment, knowing, they remember me and
suckle, desperate, at the words on my breath.
I've been tasting mouths, divining tongues, looking
for you. Let them gape at me, fall slack against the slipperiness

I press into them. I'm as much them as who
I've become. All our dreams are plasma-struck,
defenceless. I'm here in the carpark ready to spit words,
stain the gravel between these tidy, auto-locked mockeries

of our past. You'd remember if you hadn't dived
into a double-brick world of curtains and plush carpets.
Was it worth the short time you had? I've hoarded all
our words, little dried charms, collected, carried

in a pouch at my hip. I've lugged our many tongues
for so long. My fingers fret at them,
the little brown shapes, edges curled, leather-dry.
I'll fill my mouth with the withered gobbets,

bite down on what we thought was true, chew
until they start to bleed the words we shared and I
have the taste of your voice in my blood again.

# Behind Orana Takeaway

We're out of the rain, hunched around
                                    a feast
                                    five dollars worth of chips
                    ripped open on the concrete,
                            you're breathing loud vinegar snorts,
          licking your fingers with savour.

          Taliyah grins at your glister-eyed hunger,
looks at the clotted skin beneath your singlet, she asks
          to touch your scars.
                    When you don't answer she eyes me – 'How long's
                              he been deaf?'
                    My answer is another swallow of chips.

                    You're looking away at passing cars, don't see
          her question.

I watch her reach toward your scars.

          *behind the shops*

          *the smell of dirty grease*

          *rain on concrete*

          Her fingers are fearful at first
                    like your skin is molten
                              and the shiny flesh will pull away
                    sticky on her tender nails.

I'm the only one who knows your story

We're playing cricket in the rain;
you bowl
I slog;

the tennis ball fizzes over parked cars.
You turn tail and trot
out beyond the gutter.


White Holden

You don't see
the car come around our corner, your turn
tail trot steps onto the street.

White Holden
always seeing

always seeing        White Holden
your body


a candid stillness on asphalt.

The car doesn't stop, I'm the only one who hears it speed away.
You open your eyes.

Your back is a tale of gashes,
the delicate armature of your ears
has been disordered. I can't read the strange, silent
terror your mind has been thrust into.

You stand and leg it,
run without looking back
like it was you who did wrong.

For minutes I fail to follow,
enough time for you to run up a walkway
into the streets beyond.

I search, alone
I search for hours. I search until

I find you in the stormwater drain
the shadow tunnel under our streets,
we're not meant to come here.
You're bent forward, hunched
with the concrete curve. A stream of water runs
around my ankles. There's blood
leaking through the holes ripped in your shirt.

I yell an echo past your figure,
you don't turn, intent on a lithe shape

                                        nestled in your palm,
                 some charm you've given yourself into.

      I'm thirsty, thirstier than I've ever been,
    and I kneel to drink the silty water running over
your feet. I swallow what I can,
it tastes like the days we live through. I yell again,
                            my voice echoes away.

      Closer, I see movement in your hands
             a protean, reptile shimmer. You look up.
          In your palm a skink bites silently at air. I speak,
you don't answer. You're gentle, thumb
          cocked behind its neck, stroking its spine.

      You pass the skink to me,
             the heart patters against my palm
                and raindrops quiver from your hair.

I'm the only one who knows your story

      Taliyah's fingers settle on your scars, rest there
                 like it's better than chips.

    *behind the shops*

    *the smell of dirty grease*

    *rain on concrete*

You're still, biting the air,
        turning to see her words
            as she says

                    his scars feel like scales.

# White Holden

It's easier to watch a cat die
study it flipping death throes

on a neat lawn and wonder
how life keeps itself

in the terrible deportment of skin.
He's been driving for hours

this car is a confession
he can't stop speaking.

All my words are whimpering
pieces of travel-trash

down near his feet. Nothing
I can say moves beyond his eyes.

There are three bags in the back seat
and a video recorder he stole

from his parents. There must be blood
on the bumper. He keeps staring

through the windscreen. We should stop
and look. That doesn't seem possible.

The wheels keep spinning. There's a whirring
phonetics I'm trying to comprehend.

It doesn't sound like anything he'd say.
Headlights are flicking on. He gags denials

and they sound like metal on bone.
I don't know what he's saying.

In the world outside our windscreen
the asphalt is covered in bones.

There are children streaming onto the road,
balls bouncing from the trees.

# Old Gods Pass

*i.*

In the shadow of Westmead Hospital
by the playground's evening insect fret
a conclave of gods has risen

groggy from waiting room dreams,
cigarettes behind ears, tongues
sludgy with regret. They're weighing

tales of corridor dawns, time spent trembly
in wards watching the finger twitch of patients;
ferrying coffee, opening sandwiches, telling family

to sleep. They've plans for cutting –
ropes of sausage, a fundraiser in the carpark
of a local Bunnings. The manager is a believer

and heathens have money. The idea puffs
them briefly and they strut, lungs busting
with tales of rebirthed cars and front bar

transubstantiation. As they chant street lore,
their minds are free of blood counts, stents
and the respirator whisper of hospital diction.

*ii.*

Sunshine on a charred altar lures pot-bellied pagans,
their fingers scored with paper cuts, shorts pressed,

apps synched across all devices. The gods are sharing,
a red-nosed colloquy of grief: pictures of children

huffing bubbles through a morphine curtain, towering
sparkies crumpled, fretful in waiting rooms.

As the pagans flood from hardware aisles the gods
talk shop; regale weekenders with garden aspirations,

prod trolleys loaded with gleaming tools.
The heathens hear them and pause,

caught in the mess of old reign. A congregation
forms around the gods of cash in hand,

the gods of borrowed tools; as onions blacken
gods pierce fleshy snags, gods shake tongs

at the infinite. The heathens jingle change –
a show of peace – and listen to the spat and patter

of deities. There's truce in the two-way
fumbling; notes are slipped into shaken tins

and pagans mingle with gods, dripping tomato sauce,
until they are filled with unsteady faith.

# Tesla on The Crescent, Fairfield 1998

We're standing out the front of Fairfield station
in a huddle with Tesla and Lawson
waiting for the Nightride bus.

It'll pull around The Crescent, soon,
covered in splinters of glass and gobs of spit.
Kids inside breathing what's left of the night

on each other; sprawled on the seats, each one
with an unlit smoke
between their lips – it's the only play

they make at being civil. Tesla is appalled.
I pretend we've been at Delmonico's drinking
nothing but mint tea and plying ourselves

with out-of-date platitudes. Lawson talks
like he's a poet fronting a punk-a-billy band. I know
this is less than glamorous. There's a Babel of human

dialects from the punters at the rear, each face fronting
about the game they've got; declarations
even Lawson doesn't recall from his fevered benders.

Tesla scowls like they're a cabal of recalcitrant
offsiders just waiting for him to raise his arm
and will them all into righteous labour. Lawson clucks,

tongue-tuts, stoned and faux-urbane he blows
a tirade of kisses through his moustache and starts
festooning the air with nicknames. It's Tesla

who has set us on this journey, he has a bag
full of burek from Tasic, we're taking them
to his frenemy Marconi. They're a peace

offering, a grease-slimed bribe. Tesla
has finally found a site for the new
Wardenclyffe Tower, nearby; but first

it's a long ride into the city and back out
the other side. Up the Northern Beaches,
where Marconi has been secreting away patents

and scribbling intentions in his chequebook.
Like always, Tesla needs cash to float
his plan. He's been talking in sparks

for weeks, new-shining, a gleaming
amalgam of maybes; walking The Crescent,
hands in his suit pockets, coils and wire

at his fingertips. Pedestrians feel the charge of current
unreleased, the hair-lifting static of possibility.
Even Lawson listens when Tesla's mood is so

manic. We've seen the site, been taken
on excursions to the badlands behind Liverpool,
watched him cross-hatch plans on the

back of train tickets. He's sourcing steel,
looking for workers; drawings and prototypes
riddle his mind. He can see his tower rising from the trees

a metal net for clairvoyance, straining meaning
from air, broadcasting submerged voices.
He tells us, air is hard with the current of anecdote,

the convulsion of words, consonants clarifying
into meaning. We're living in a confluence
of language, a tongue with many

forks. We rub coins to make a noise.
Each of us has unspent fables wearing
holes in our pockets. We jingle them across

the city and onto the strange northern roads
toward Marconi and conversation of all things
electric. We arrive as morning starts to bleed mercury

along the horizon. Marconi is dressed as a tradie;
actual overalls and a tan,
concrete caked boots. Tesla hands the burek

over and they stand in the doorway, greasy paper
between them, a faded scent. Marconi leads
into the kitchen and we sit to watch him carve

his meat burek with the daintiness of a queen.
He chews and laughs with his mouth full,
Lawson is on the nod. We watch. Marconi

is dressed for trade but his face is all accounts
and balance sheets. Tesla describes
his intentions in a jigsaw of twenty

sketched-over bus tickets. The cross-hatchings
dream themselves into alignment, he breathes
the yellow mist of invention. And Marconi

leans back from his meal, spreads his legs
beneath the table, shakes his head.

# Woman Feeding Magpies

'...*magpies are fearless defenders of their territory, often driving more imposing creatures from the area they have claimed...*'

The End will arrive
clattering bells and crowned
with an upturned ice cream tub,
ridiculous and desperate,
knowing his charms don't work on you,
mind addled by all the times
he has tried and missed –
collecting the innocents from your brood:
      son, husband
      sister, daughter.

Even he feels guilt
when death taps the wrong shoulder.

He waits on the footpath outside your house,
his clawed feet
covered in green ants. Your maggies sense blood
on him; the corpse-meat under his fingernails
lures like rotten mince. They swoop –
upending the tub on his head,
stealing the bells looped around his arm.
Two attack his ankles
until he's tripping retreat
toward the roadside.

You follow, bend with a joint-crack,
pick up the ice cream tub and limp
toward the gutter. He's jerky with nerves, yet
when he speaks there's a plunderer's poise.
He takes the tub from your hand and says:

*soon the magpies will leave your yard;*
*they'll carry rocks*
*build mounds on the footpath*
*touch beaks with their kin.*
*soon you'll wake & they'll be gone,*
*no mimic voices;*
            *no chirps of found & lost*
*no swoops protecting you*
*their wings will welt the air*
*feathers will fall from the sky*

*this is when you die*

*a blind man at your bedside*
*two children at your feet*
*my mistakes jostling to meet you*

You don't answer.
There's a lottery ticket in your apron pocket,
in the kitchen
there's a phone about to ring.
When you turn, his voice is a truck passing –
the sound a cloud makes being borne.

# Four Children, Fifty-Seven Envelopes

Tonight, at the back fence, on my knees
in the bed where pumpkin vines
have turned to ogres,
I'm hiding teeth, enamelled seeds,
two knuckles deep
in the cold earth.

Grandma had a drawer full of milk teeth
folded away in envelopes.
A cluster of ballpoint dates and names
in the place where the stamp should go.
They only know one home. It feels traitorous
to take them away, pack them in a strange drawer.

They've chewed life
into her sons and daughters,
been knocked out of heads
in backyard footy games,
bitten into apples,
fallen between fingers into freedom.

I know they're only teeth
they could never taste,
all they had was force.
They shouldn't mean anything

but I can imagine them grinning.
I can see my mother fussing
a clot of bone from her gum.
They deserve a place to settle, rest

from eavesdropping. This ground
has a taste for lost words; I've already buried
three wedding rings in the soil,
my fingers crave dirt.

# Goodbye, a Premonition

The first voice we hear is blue flashing lights
your mouth opens and sirens appear

> Trains yellow-nose a hole in the summer storm
> every minute there's a tremor

If it rains hard enough    rib bones
flood from drains    the cardboard city starts to melt

> Eels flip on sidewalks and all
> we remember seeps from leaves

Night dogs yelp our indiscretions
across the city's tiled back

> Saviours arrive    first a van
> then the promise of a bed for the night

Their words are a mouth in motion    friend is a hand
on the arm    belief is the way you shape my name

> Our vows are lifted from the menu at Happy Cup
> your smile comes in three flavours

We're hiding from rain    clouds in our ears
pinkies bound with sugar syrup

> The worthy queue to drag combs through our hair
> coax us with saintly intercessions

They shine a torch on your eyelashes
hold a mirror to your lips     you're an empty straw

                              A body outlasting     the need to breathe
                                   their fingers dial up the future

I don't remember the name you had
before we met in this place

                                   the alphabet they need to mark
                                        your position on a list

Make you another life  floating electronic
through space     into sieved arms

                              Beneath the overpass     I huddle
                                   up against the pylons

Scratch pictograms into cement
break soil

                              The dirt is loose     I dig     fingers taut
                                   brothers and sisters thigh to thigh

Hit the water table     black sludge
identity worn from fingertips

                                   Body streaked     shovel hands
                              slicing the mute earth into noisy clumps

# Southdown Place

be a ghost gum rising from the waterhole in each heart

               tromp footsteps
                      where the sky should start
          wash your face in the Georges River
                  wet visions     dashed across eyes
                yabby-sludge twitching in hair

be the steel and flint
      flaring with each stride    be hair chopped Mohican

    huff petrol at stars

be fingers clutching a jar of heat haze
          brain ruched with fumes
          body in a broken-window room
mattress dragged from the footpath    listen
                   to the blister on whisper lips

be keening flames and warped light    the crackle
                             before ash
                  a yes
             cast    burning from hands
      lay back on the mattress

       watch flames
   roil the ceiling

feel the heat begin to bear

blink a scatter of cockatoo feathers at the light

be the doorway exhaling ash      be a face painted with flame

be the wind as it condemns

be a siren singing soot from the sky

# The Upper Room

# With Chris Ofili in The Upper Room

From darkened walls, Ofili's monkeys conspire, their eyes
trail as we move from painting to painting. Dreams bristle
in the half light. You know their pack vision, smell paws
festered with glimmering elephant dung. Our animal spirit

feels the heat of their jungle blood, strength of coiled
freedom, painted primate eyes, rhesus hearts. We are
footsteps in their ears, we drift awe-silent, colour to colour.
Their resinous palpitations heat our hearts, nerves of glitter

reach for us. To be still is not enough, they strain to escape.
When we leave they uncouple from the linen. Lacquer
and oil crackle as they slide from the walls, find their feet,
and clamber cavalier onto the street. Without knowing

we lead away from the city turrets, across Grand Union
canal. We breathe concrete air, feel brittle sun, I read
valedictions between your blunt teeth, we see orchids
in the foliage. Around us the monkeys move, preening

painted fur, twinkling in London sun. Their chatter
sounds human, thin tongues lick the city air, sequinned
lips try to grin; like us, they want to ride the tube,
find the edge of this city. Across Islington footpaths,

between cars. We jump the barrier at Angel, scurry down
the escalator. They forage for colours in the tiled underworld,
nails scratch brittle hiss-clicks in the tunnels, weave glitter
between passengers. The doors slop a seal and we ride

as the monkeys search beneath seats, swing from rails, claw
joyfully at the windows. After Highgate we shoot into light,
the monkeys shriek, sun and blue reflected in their milky eyes.
With each station, city falls away, the sky stretching to welcome

us. I see tawny fur sprout on your neck, feel the alacrity
of strange blood. The monkeys know us. Their tails twitch
interest; our lungs fill with mountain mist, rhesus visions of wire
coops, scar furrows, unfamiliar hearts beating in bandaged ribs.

They tell us all. The doors open at High Barnet; a flock of birds
crackle the sky and we move, eyes up, betraying our monkey
hearts. They scamper and we gleefully ditch our humanity,
chasing, a pack running to know the tremble in our ribs.

# Sweet Tooth In The Afterlife

I've been hearing a hum under the floorboards.
I've been peeking with a torch,
levering at the boards with a crowbar.
When light gets in, there's all kinds of ransom:
ticket stubs, busted plastic toys,
the dried shells of dead cockroaches
– ingredients for inner city incantations –

and deeper, the hum is louder.
Bees nudge my arm as they move in dark air,
their hive is hidden
warm with insect tat-tat.

Honey has a message, I know,
we can hoard it for centuries
in claypots, like the Egyptians,
have a secret stash
in case one of us conjures
a sweet tooth in the afterlife.

I'm taking the hive from beneath the boards,
I'll tear it into chunks
and send a hunk of honey comb
to all the places we lived
every half remembered address;
each chunk wrapped in a faded property report
bound in bubble wrap, sealed in a post pack.

There'll be strangers unwrapping the bundles,
looking for scissors, cutting tape, licking pulp
from shaking hands; all the slip-sweetness,
bits of bee, workers mandibles,
shape gathered from the dust.

If another person could know
the parts of us that have shimmered
through crevices,
the years in wax:
our shudder of passage –
a bee banking ambivalent
through trails of pollen;

me at your side
truth cinched in a kiss
my doubt a wax skeleton
my love a hundred pitchers of honey.

*Last line borrowed from Jack Gilbert's* The Forgotten Dialect of the Heart.

# Babies in Her Hair

At stations you'll be offered bags of walnuts
through the train window. Take them,
split the shell with a pocket knife. Share
them with the ancient woman who peels
boiled eggs with arthritic intensity.

As her blackened finger casts shell away
she will reveal the ridged silver ring
above her knuckle. Touch it for luck.
When her son returns with bottles of beer
take one. The plains will keep moving,

windows will rattle, air will thicken. Step
into the corridor, slide the cabin
door closed. The horizon is an eyelash
on the haze. Lean your head out the window
into the air, smell the diesel tang.

In the next cabin they'll be playing cards,
watch, play if you must, there's time
to pass and not much left to lose. Drink
their brandy, it will quarry your doubts.
To leave, show them cigarettes

and step into the corridor. When
they follow, offer smokes, watch
their embers burning. They'll talk
around you, exhaling mountains
into the sky. The plains will keep

moving. You'll be held at the border
as the chassis is changed. Don't
sleep, your dreams will flare with strange
sounds. The border guard will come,
declarations hidden in his hat,

he will ask for documents. Your papers
are written in a hand you know, ink
the colour of a daughter's hair. The city
is not in sight. Soon you'll be locked in your cabin.
Breathe with the old woman as she combs babies

from her hair. They'll drop, fine as insects,
to the ground, translucent embryos
in motion, crawling for the gap
beneath the door, a subtle swarm
disappearing into the sunlit corridor.

# Dress Uniform

There is a woman screaming
from my balcony, naked
breasts quivering with rage.

She has been tender; in bed we were
a heart-shaped question, her ribs a ripple
beneath my fingers, knees bent toward

the edge of peaceful half-sleep. My euros
well spent. No longer. Now she yells
the taste of me from her mouth.

She has my keys in her hand, holding
them like a broken trophy, my uniform
in the other, slack and bodiless. Her lips

spit the grit of my name at a growing
crowd. I feel the sting of their hunger
rising from the street. She casts

my uniform at their mouths and I
imagine my chevrons trampled, torn.
The first rock is a surprise, through

the window; they mean her no harm.
I hear their voices chanting the slogan
that follows me. Another rock, glass

on the carpet; I no longer have the will
to harm them. I hear the cheer from below
as she throws my keys from the balcony.

They must dazzle through the air; the last
brazen part of me. My hands are empty;
shirtless I wait for footsteps from the hall.

## Suvorov Square

At night, novels stroll on gravel
pathways, whispers and powdered
cheeks lifting with each white
breath. Their confessions are fur-lined,
necessary, worn to the thread.

Eugene tears a letter into wishes that trail
at his feet, Pushkin follows aiming
his quill. Anna Karenina sits with her daughter,
picking strands in a cat's cradle; Tolstoy nibbles
a banana and tries to ignore their laughter.
Raskolnikov badgers his shoe laces
thinking of the coffee house where
Dostoyevsky waits, texting rhapsodies to his bookie.

In the morning, their mute footsteps
are raked over by sturdy women. Nearby,
oblivious children parse the ribs of fallen
leaves, collecting handfuls to flutter and crackle
at the hush between each rasping scrape.

# An Excess of Consciousness

Gertrude knows

how to collaborate

where to buy coffee

and pleasantries

that are repeated

repeated repeated

worn into the realm of now

worn until they are pure being

a muscle trained to cast words

a tongue dipped in silver

# Malik's Mongoose

Malik runs Three Card Monte
from an upturned crate. In the rubbish
end of Seven Sisters Rd – junk,
counterfeit designer shell-suits, derros
squeaking trolleys over rotten fruit.

Splinters in his swift fingers,
embalmed mongoose by his side.
I learned fast not to challenge his cryptic hands
or chase the disappearing cloak he drew tight
before he ran into the Seven Sisters crowd.

Now, I play second patter, pale clown
in a laugh-tragedy, dropping a fiver, winning loudly,
heckling the glassy mongoose eyes,
petting the coarse fur, cackling Irish luck, creating
the suspect furrow of sound players discover.

There's a crumpled fortune in sweaty pockets
awaiting the graceful fingers of liberation. We
roust the crowd. Numbers mean players,
means money, means one more chance
to slip this infernal knot.

His patter is perfect. 'Malik, like the Parisian
market; Malik with the gypsy face.' Points
at his stuffed mongoose. 'One touch, sir,
for luck.' A player steps forward, drawn
into the web. Lips move, fingers arch.

# By Mesurado River

There's a barricade in our city, strange camps
struck in co-opted building sites, megaphone
shrieks. I trail antiseptic through concrete
dust. We lumber, bags on our feet, dragging static,

door to door. People run from us, sandals
clicking, they scream through t-shirt balaclavas.
In the back of my truck a child is curled,
foetal on a square of cardboard. A boy sipping

last hope from a dry thumb. At each threshold
we pray. Rumour is the new liturgy. Alley news
is a whisper, information a growl, we speak
through the muzzle of fear. I watch

for red eyes, the gastric stink of night
sweat; Doctors speak around me –
a dialect of green gloves, protective goggles.
We know there are too many bodies.

In each face I see our past; needle fingers,
fishbones secret under my tongue, hoarding
the gut of nets dropped by the tide,
unravelling squalls to knot again and recast

over the cockled ripple of this river. No longer
am I able to follow orders. Along the barricade
street dogs weave witness; snarls
covered in fur. They've been eating the dead.

I must return. My mother sleeps beyond the line,
bags of clothes by her bed, dust adrift
over toys and the potions of her life. The bugs
weep her organs out of shape. She sweats

the sap of trees we have never known.
I run to the barricade where I bartered beside her;
toppled market stalls, splintered
remnants coiled with razor wire. I am another

question a-skulk at the frayed border. How
can we not kiss the dying, feel their delirious
labour on our forehead? I weave
under the cordon. My mother has a sister's voice,

tenderness with fangs, eyes for wrongdoing,
even blind with fever she knows
I have come to cover her,
to slip shoes from her feet. All her life

she has strewn scales at the river edge,
caught water-cool jewels on the tips of her fingers
and lifted them silver into the light. At the river,
I cross the bank, her body in a bag. Death rasp

still on my cheek. The shore smells of engine fluid,
rancid sand. A brackish tide laps, the moon
draws a crooked line. Before morning I will
return my mother to the coal belly of the Mesurado.

# Basketball in Davao

three points drop through the chain net
beyond the court a shot clock falters
the bodies we've been arch
pass at moonlight
& fall between end lines

your hand rips holes in darkness
right arm orchestrating lay ups
hawk's hunger when you land
chain net rattling applause
you're screening shadows

street cat & raptor
miscegenation's miracle
barefoot for hours
feathers tufting from your toes
swinging in the space between asphalt & hoop

somehow judge & jury find you here
Pinoy Rock spilling from car windows
makeshift court girded with insect noise & accusation
trial judge pointing a pistol
jury sweating adobo

they've torn your clothes to protestations
you're naked on knees at the top of the key
hands open to people who fill holes with your unborn children
pockets spilling the arcane & intimate
evidence unruly on the asphalt

i balance a ball on my hip
watch a final jeer tremble across your lips
there's a gunshot gavel
a second shot & the court unravels
jury & prosecution twist away from the key

words for this run palm to palm
how your soft hands thread a pass across the free throw line
how bullet holes say your name
how the back of your head opens like a humid void
& your mouth adorns the air with jewels
&

# Matsutake: Life and Non-Life

## i.
### The Pickers

past a particular agri-city's industrial strobing
pickers camp in tents
muddled in sleeping bags
breathing air against their better judgement

levitating on financial promise
watching barometers and mapping daylight
waiting for the search to begin

dogs nose pine needles
foraging for blooms
lopsided fungi
fleshy stems scavenged from the earth

## ii.
### The Pickers

every morning my father licks his teeth
as he wakes
as we move

in the dawn he unfolds a map
today we search the northern quadrant
grids are coded in dark pencil
we've started to alternate trips into the pines

the back seat of his car is packed
with three plastic tubs
hessian cloth over a tumble of awkward shapes

he's careful to keep it locked
and guarded
dogs chained to each door handle
shaking messages across the earth

### iii.
### The Pickers

bred in the space between
tent and trailer
my hand hurling empty cans
at the road

my breath is pine mulch
my bones golden
my flesh the colour of broken branches
i speak in twenty dialects
dogs nuzzle me into daylight

mother painted my bones
gave me a dogs-tooth necklace
said we're all spies in the forest
eyes fixed on needles
shifting in the undergrowth

*iv.*
**The Buyers**

yesterday i didn't ring
your buzzer
there are many things i should never say
we don't speak

my words are mushrooms
wrapped in paper

my apology white
gilled
ready to be sliced
i hold them in my arms
my finger on your buzzer
the elevator is full of autumn
pine needles

i'll brush the dirt off with you
look for a recipe
wait for you to draw the knife

we could cut ourselves back to shape
cook a conversation from silence
rebuke the meals we've failed to share

*v.*
**The Pickers**

fingers have individual rituals
pluck coins from the ground
work to hold another girdling year from throats

humans grimace through the web of commerce
without knowing they touch eyes
through the thin tent tarp

and try to believe in fingers
greased with rolling tobacco
the white knuckle
love has held at their cheek


*vi.*
**The Buyers**

i'm a *gaijin* and this country
will never say my name
i've drilled myself from friendship

tuned myself away from possibility
there's only the sound of our kids growing
like trees their lives shape

and branch into the rugby players we regret
the door swings as they leave
all that's left is the hollow we've carved


*vii.*
**The Buyers**

i shouldn't have said what i said

your bedroom is a living room
is full of the things
we promised to hoard
when we cook it's on the flare of a 5000 yen hotplate

i carry six months of what i could have been
my arms are tired of being
alone
i come bearing ingredients for a second life

one mushroom for forgiveness
one mushroom for another minute
in your doorway

*viii.*
*The Pickers*

the earth floats in poisonous air
when we clip our toenails
diners feel it three borders away
there is nothing to stop us from talking
except the sound food makes
circling the globe
we have acres longing within us
a terabyte of sky reflected in our eyes


*ix.*
*The Buyers*

i have not seen the inside of his coffin
plastic has rubbed itself to death
there are still numbers i left scratched
on the wall

the place always smells of tea
and washing
barely dry

i recognise the buzzer
my finger knows the shape
somewhere above my mother shifts

this place is an ending
my accent has been uncovered
there is nothing in this world

i have not spoken
i translate flames and wind
wash my hands in concrete


*x.*
*The Pickers*

bent hand above
the spine a dog moves
through the forest

we are glue-eyed creatures
on the scent of longing
asleep in plastic bags

breathing condensation
nothing frightens us
not even the threat forgiveness makes

## xi.
### The Pickers

there is nothing to kill here
what lives has no breath
gills like a fin-less fish

we're people fighting for a campsite
knives hidden in our pockets
ignoring the way our fingers match

don't bring me here again
persevering with the present
stalking hunks of nothing

## xii.

forests have turned to pine
innovation spluttering rationales
in the golden hour of agri-corp

we're share-breathing the choke of monoculture
a combine harvester with wifi
our food chain a broken question mark

commerce is a knot
the sky is charred
each belly filled with coal

we don't know
why spores hold shape
how the furrow roots make through soil

the cover of nettles
allow matsutake's tarnished veil
to bless tongues with answers

taste sings many songs
desire studies through the net
humans come without metal edges

the wicker-world cannot hold them
they continue to have children
continue to curse Facebook friends

drink tea in the shade
wait for mushrooms to grow

# Sol de los Muertos

we woke in the afternoon     by sunset i'd shaved your head
  Fawcett-flicks trembled in my hand

   i promised something    feudal       loyalty immutable

     you fled Monterey      eyes doused with mist
pockets stuffed with hair   ears ringing with Spanish Castle Magic

i should've kept your flicks    they'd be tarred with menthol smoke

or something at least
something better
'cause now
i'm here
at the most dire terminus on the west coast

& a guy in a Lakers singlet is poking my shoulder
     & i'm waking up    & he's
  handing me a newspaper   pointing to a bus   i run

  paper in hand    on the bus i stretch out the front page
      i shouldn't recognise you        now
twenty years later   except  time never wore the culprit smirk
      from your face

sunlight isn't strong enough to stop the thought of you
    perching on my lap    you come reborn
     wrists exposed to dawn   pale fingernail blades
        questions notched on your inner arm

your apathetic tongue
glazing my lips        careless

i watch concrete buildings        feel a knot of white noise
try not to read the words i've seen                you're missing

not news itself        except part of you has been found
        an arm
                severed above the elbow
the fingers printed        & pointing to our petty past

# LA River: 94% Concrete 6% Water

LA River is a trickle
desperation cutting the counterculture smog,
this pre-dawn it's serrated, we watch for melody
on the surface.

All we know
about the river comes from films
& the screeching danger of Los Santos.

Stormwater drains pock the concrete banks,
circular caverns broad enough
to house a convention of misfits.

Some of us are sifting
last night through sunglasses. We've forgotten
our names, there's a guitar player
without a guitar,
a boy beatboxing his way
to the lip of the stormwater drain.
We're huddled in this echoing cylinder,
desert sand rough in every word we say.

Twice a day we keen prophecies.

*Waters are coming,*
*there's a pulse along Santiago Peak's antenna-speared spine.*
*Inland snows have been melting;*
*the sea is finger-waving at desert sands, there's too much sting in the sunlight,*
*hills are on fire*

*we're caught in the middle –*
*January's blue fingers in our pockets.*

We've all been riffing on this concrete river
some of us with a Bell Creek back beat
some hyping Arroyo Calabases.
We've got cheeks full of syllables.   We're straining them
between teeth
catching leaves
ants
orange pips.

The roads start to fill. 18-wheelers rumble
over the high-pitched whine of trail bikes.

Fault lines wait to kiss this city off the coast.
We want to stand on Hyperion Bridge,
watch the hills burn and live stream the end of times, see ash
falling from the flushed morning.

We're small players,
minstrels. We tune guitars
to hide the sound of electricity twitching.
We vibrate
and talk our bodies into silence.

Before the sun finds today's answer
water will come flooding down the drains
waist deep              with a cargo of crimes.

My shoes are off
I'm walking from the stormwater drain
over the edge, down the concrete slope
and into the city's trashed-up arterial.

There's no rain in the place we've invented
or there's too much rain and fire
that can't be extinguished.

# Netherfallen

garble at mirrors
flick as flowflakes
face on flock wallpaper
Xanax fingertips on velour
narrow avenue of addled resistance

first son to swallow
the words on a tongue

three names of netherfallen
secrets enough to fill the time

motor muttering
cloven chest
face unravelled from bone
glass
chip packets
cola bottle on the asphalt

shivering flies
roadkill
litters from aloft

whirlwords
discarded rubbings of a generation

confession
the only lyrics
isges to isges erde to erde

*This poem contains words from* Finnegans Wake *by James Joyce.*

# Last of the Barbary Lions

*ii.*

There's no Hippocratic Oath for vets;
in this world a man is what morals make him. I'm indentured to a thug
with a pocket full of mobile phones,
two weeks into a handshake pact of pills and powders.

I've been paid to wait, collude
in the plaza haze, my feet
kicking alleys of August wind.

Perched on a stool in Calle Melo's limestone glower,
watching ocean and sea blur in the Strait.
I'm doling tablets to door knocks,
cutting chorizo with a necktie knife; listing
on a nightly lullaby of horse tranquillisers.

I breathe in the dry air, breathe out
a stem of opioid desire
and settle at the bar,
petals in my mouth.

This is my last night swallowing broken Spanish,
feet on the solstice line
a half step ahead of winter shade.

The ferries from Morocco
are on endless loop, red hulls
split sky and sea.

*iii.*
In a warehouse on the far side of town,
beyond the dunes,
the heat buckles around
a canvas bag of meds. My next stop
when word comes.

And when I flee
even the jawbone of this harbour won't utter my name.

*iv.*
At Café Pensione,
eyes bent on evening, I wait for gambling
border guards to pass under the archway
into old town, their footfalls announce evening.

*vi.*
My phone will ring. They will call.

There's a car we'll share to Jerez
and in the back seat I'll examine the cubs;
one will be bleeding from a nostril.

*v.*
From the darkening alley each shadow hides
a furred bundle.
Lion cubs are en route
from the Atlas Mountains, they've flinch-dreamed
across deserts,
lapped water drawn from stagnant dams.

Lion cubs don't purr, they strip bones,
rubble growl, paw feline terror in cloth. If they come to me

they'll be bundled against the warmth of a border guard's chest,
needled to sleep, tarnished gold
fur barely breathing.

*vii.*
Headlights lean a path
through night. Palm fronds
search the sky for a moon. I have a word
written on my arm. We're hours
from Jerez.
There are numbers to call.

*i.*
Someone has tattooed LIONS on my forearm.
I'm trying to wash it off in the Atlantic.
My sunglasses are salt splashed
I'm rancid with thirst, my cut-off jeans
flap in the waves, the only shirt I own is a story
the Levante tells my skin.

I limp a bent line to the day bars,
they're cracking first beers and playing
Macklemore on repeat through portable speakers. I nod
to the hepped-up flow. I know every nook
on this earth is white-washed with pallid graffiti.
We tap fingers to what we despise.

# Shape of the Earth

It starts with crystal powder at our feet, cracked geodes
on the terrace in Tangier. Quartz-lined segments split
along ancient seams. We reach at pieces and under our fingers
the broody guise forgets shape. You gather
a sack of fragments, what we can carry, and lead to the port.

On the ferry, gliding through Levante's sharp breath,
we moult quartz shards. Our unborn daughter
kicks and fossicks in the geodes' huddled chill.
Across the Strait, palm fronds squint at the last
hours of day; they've spent years bent,

rating each bluster. We came to this place
trailing a parade of wind-blown polyglots,
tongues dashed with Sanlúcar. Here our hopes
speak patois echoes, we walk ghost grooves
in limestone alleys; feel the purl and release

within you, our shape, passing.
We stop in the square, a salsa band begins
their night-bird squabble, stallholders
meddle the position of wares.
Our unborn daughter runs a patchwork,

until she's drawn away
by a fast-fingered tout
braiding hair into coloured stems.
She points to threads, we watch as the silver
strands are plaited through her hair. This place is becoming

our skin; soon windblown tarps will whip-flap the sound of our days,
we'll mark the season with quills,
fibreglass masts, the tracks kitesurfers drag
toward waves. Our nights are lost in plazas
listening to deserters ride a whitewater hush toward dawn.

Our daughter
dreams through the noise, her braid
caught between fingers. It holds for almost
long enough, and when the unspooling comes
it's a never-ending strand of coloured cotton,

a palm of lion roars,
Moroccan mint, fur of camels, quartz dust –
all spilling thick and bloody between your fingers.

# Abruption – near the bear, northern

king tides rush the harbour
at the shoreline    i measure currents
plot temperatures

like me    water
doesn't hold shape    or settle to being

there are days    i come gasping and slick from the deep
twisting history from my sides
i feel the lift of ancient gills on my neck
i long to return to silver
a single fish in the ever-moving cloud

i was born swaddled in a boat's ribs    riding the Beaufort Sea swell
snow trailing from the sky    mother knotted my umbilical
cast our placenta into the water
polar cod twisted a silver glove around the pouch    mouthed
clots of mother-blood
as they unfurled the her that made me    turned us part water
part fish    feed for the school who held us in their oily blood

i'm there    in the bend of waves    cresting to air
cutting patterns beneath riddled Arctic ice    sliding    knife edge
silvery through water
i breathe out holes
i see the shape of space and the eye blink in every cell

oceans exhale the history of ice    clouds conceal a breach
waves gnaw a new waterline    and i stand on shore
gills fluttering at the sky    there's east wind on my cheeks

gaseous ancestors released from ice and returning to the atmosphere
breath of neanderthals    slime of crawling fish    spit of lizard-bird

stretching in the air                    i measure
the hole against myself to see if it fits a part of me that lives fluid
the sure shape of hindsight
it's only the familial strings of evolution that tie me to land
i watch ice calve jigsaw pieces into the sea

polar bears adrift and bellowing            a bear knows love
their mighty claws err warnings in the broken Arctic shelves

i'm bound to water my spine feels the ocean's liquid palpitations
rushing a message along lateral lines        churning Beaufort Gyre

my shape slides    one scale    in the silver of an articulating cloud
krill in mouth            each tail swish
evolution's wake

# Hand in Glove

flex a fist      blow your mist of winter words
into a leather glove          we've set course

for the sun-scribed cloud        our bus ride mapped in fine
nibbed biro        a pattern of ley-lines inked

on the surface of your gloves          you trace capillary
streets across threadbare fingers

check off monuments marked on the pleated palm
out the window gulls        unveil  euphoric from ledges

and totter against wind        plunging in great Trafalgic arcs
across the span of our window        they beat

the shape of clouds into our eyes and we let them fill us
with Marylebone's concrete breath    each bus ride is a chance

to huddle        Highgate Hill on the rise from your thumb
Spaniards Road wild with horses across your wrist

Camden in the cinch of your love line      the knuckle-bump
mistakes of N1        each finger stretched supple to a river crossing

we watch each other with questions          you wear a ring
outside your glove        mindfully attentive to new anatomy

on the skyline          if you clench your fingers right
you can touch my jugular with St Pauls        hold me

with the Thames      i lean back      top deck    front seat
on the 59 over Waterloo Bridge and just accept the gentle pressure

my pulse a river     and your fingertips     breathless for Brixton

# Lampedo

## Night of the warriors

On the night your one-breasted warriors
came across the hill, we were a city
acquiescent. Half-alive shamblers,

well-meaning brick-buyers camped mute
in row upon row of cold terraces, waiting
to be delivered from our stale flesh.

The battle was short. We fell at a touch.
In the fox-mist blown from your lungs,
warriors sliced our city tongues and licked

us bloodless. Your Amazonian sisters
plundered a few febrile hours. At dawn, only
you remained. I rose with the mark of your hair

in my fist. At the window there was barrenness
astounding; a city eclipsed. In the silence,
I claimed a feather from behind your ear,

nestled near bone, tucked to thin skin;
fletching for an arrow. It was my first favour,
gifted while your mind was free of battle.

We were still molten. Your bow unstrung,
quiver shameless on the floor. I am
no warrior. Against the glass, I murmur

incantations lifted from the spines of novels
and wait to run this feather between us.

## The fox earth you give

In the nights following, your fox
friends find us; they hunger

through the mist, nuzzle at your side
longing for use. You must leave,

there is little time for our secret dance.
On the dawn of your first departure

a fox drifts arrogant, aware of the game
in play. You draw an arrow and loose

it into mist where it finds a thankful
whimper. Hunter-sure, you stride

into the heavy air and return
with a fox-bundle. Your forearms

let the coarse fur to my chest;
she will be protector, eyes

in city mist, screech in throat,
leader at shin. There is an arrow

in her side, blood on her fur,
each breath is softer. She wears

the eyes you bring hunting. Her body
knows this city; she is my keeper

and when you return we will be
strong and burnished with hunger.


## After too long

You come from the dark with durian on your face,
your bow slung across your chest. Our streets reek

of desire, the furies hang from power lines,
hair in braids, their snake tongues whisper

bitter delight. I have been waiting for this moon,
it has been too many nights since your last hunt.

The fox you left to guard me aches for another wound;
my hand no longer soothes her. I feel the arrowhead we left

under her fur, I remember cutting the shaft away,
leaving her ribs lumpen. Now I trail her vixen

scream through this city; across Highgate Bridge
riding a belly of mist, her sidestep trot

padding morse on the asphalt, she nuzzles
bins, lingering in street light. Her ear lifts

to hear your polyglot riddles, the fickle crunch
of leaves underfoot, and soon, the faultless

path of an arrow, a message you are near.


## A night again

We carry the fox-bundle, tend her wound,
guide her whimpers to a blanket earth.

In the darkness I touch your heel, follow
the thin gesture of achilles. Between

my fingers your skin is supple as bronze,
fiery and unformed. We devour the night,

listening for tight fox breaths. By morning
she has wept bone ink through her bandage.

She stirs into human ambivalence. At the door,
you stroke her fur, press a pouch of rocks

into the animal heat of her pelt; feel her teeth
against your bare knuckles. She is us,

through to the rough of her asphalt tongue.


## Your visits never last

My queen, you fly from Heathrow
with a fake passport between your teeth

and an enigma in your eye. Our fox is
bandaged, arrowhead in her skinny

haunch, my convalescent. I don't know
if your tears are for me or her. She will

scratch and bite the bandage from her leg;
whimper weeks away at your leaving.

I'll be tapping my teeth with a teacup,
trying to draw you from water stains

on the walls; you're a vision hidden
in every shape. My silent shamble

with the vapours of this city is over. I
promise voice to the chant of you unsaid

on my lips. Your breath has filled my lungs,
my skin will fly under your nails.

## Feathers and chalcedony

I have your feather behind my ear
and the pouch you gifted, unclutched

from the heat of your sternum. Inside
are chunks of jasper, obsidian, chert

from them I pick the shape of my first
arrowhead. Our fox sleeps in her blanket

earth; she waits for the strength
to shepherd me through our streets.

We both know you have flown to obscure
seasons; to a bed that takes your weight

from me, to sheets that steal a scent
from your pulse. I knap arrow heads

and bundle them for your return; razor
splinters prickle my fingers. I'm not the hunter

you are; there is no bow, no knife in my belt.
I will wait for the sun to move behind clouds;

watch for the sundial in clocks; tell myself
this is nothing; the lost minutes are shadowless.

# Acknowledgements

Thanks to the editors of the world, particularly the editors of the following publications, who have supported my work:

Meanjin – *Angelo* (*Angelo* received third place in The 2014 Dorothy Porter Poetry Prize)

Cordite – *Blackberry Caliphate; Kuala Lumpur 1977: Prawn Heads, Oil Rigs and Infidelity; Emperor of 32 Bella Vista Drive*

The London Magazine – *Through the Witch Window*

Verity La. – *Monsoonal Light of Our Childhood*

Minor Literature[s] – *Tropical Storm Danielle: Night Surfing*

Island Magazine – *Hamburg*

Blue Pepper – *Suvorov Square*

Liminal, Hermes 2014 – *Dress Uniform*

Snorkel – *Malik's Mongoose*

Liminal, Hermes 2014 – *Streets Have Shadows*

The Glasgow Review of Books – *Life Savers*

Tincture – *Train to Quakers*

The Glasgow Review of Books – *Reunion – Our Suburban Lingua*

The Disappearing (Red Room Poetry) – *Behind Orana Takeaway*

Dazzled, University of Canberra Poetry Prize Anthology 2014 – *With Chris Ofili in The Upper Room*

Newcastle Poetry Prize Anthology 2016 – *By Mesurado River*

Once Wild, Newcastle Poetry Prize Anthology 2014 – *Lampedo*

Burning Ink Press – *Last of the Barbary Lions; in any city, in every tongue, we walk toward the heat of morning; LA River: 94% Concrete 6% Water*

Spry – *Four Children, Fifty-Seven Envelopes*

Stilts – *A Cheekbone For You To Climb Over*

Mikrokosmos Journal – *Babies in Her Hair*

Noble/Gas Qtrly – *Shape of the Earth; Basketball in Davao*